What
I Didn't Know

Tebaliah Holmes

Acknowledgement

Although I did come up with this book idea and potential series on my own, it's not all about me. It was Jacob Murphy and his team that made my vision come to life.

From the cover, the edits, and the trailer. I owe them a big thank you. I did not think anyone would believe it was a good idea, but they did. While I was writing the first manuscript, I did not tell anyone, like friends or family. Even though that's the case, there are people in my life who influence me to do better. People like my father, Leonard, my mother, Capucina, my brothers, Tracy and Brian, my cousins Vernell and Lamamie. There are so many more, but these people have only ever wanted me to succeed and do good in this world. I don't know where I would be without their support.

Thank you, everyone.

Dedication

I dedicate this book to my sister, Savannah. I will always remember how you used to dress me up and do my hair when I was younger. I know it seemed like I hated it but I didn't know it was because you cared for me so much. You treated me like the pretty doll you knew I was. I only wish I could see myself from your point of view. I was a reflection of you. If only you knew how envious I was of your beauty growing up. The funny thing is whatever flaws you saw in yourself, I saw the opposite. It was perfection when I looked at you. Thank you for teaching me how to treat myself and know my self-worth. You are my inspiration, my friend, and my role model. I love you forever and always.

Table of Contents

Acknowledgement i

Dedication ii

Part 1 1

Part 2 8

Part 3 15

Part 1

My name is Tebaliah. No, it does not roll off the tongue naturally, but that's what makes it special. It is a unique name, a name that stands out to whoever hears it being called. I always loved my name because it is mentioned in the Bible, and having such a name made me feel special, I guess. There was something powerful about carrying a name with meaning; it almost felt sacred at times. I mean, I always got compliments on my name left and right - from friends, teachers, and even strangers I met.

It was the kind of name that people paused on to admire the entirety of it. That was enough for me. Having a beautiful name was enough. At least, it was when I was younger.

I was just a kid, though. Life was simple, and my world was small. But everything changed when I was six years old, in the middle of my first-grade year. We moved to a city outside of Houston called Pearland. At the time, Pearland felt like a contradiction - it seemed so small but yet so big. The streets over there were a lot wider than I was accustomed to; the houses were tall, and the place seemed like a new unknown waiting to be discovered. Six-year-old Tebaliah was figuring out what it meant to start over.

Suddenly, things changed for me. The move brought about new feelings for me. I started to actually pay attention to my appearance, my skin color and my hair mainly. I don't think before this, I had ever focused on these things that were just parts of me, things I had never questioned. But now, at my new school, these things that made me into me felt like differences that set me apart.

At that point in time, at my new school, there were not as many girls with my brown skin color and my curly hair. Now, my mother always made sure I looked pretty and groomed, especially my hair. She always took pride in it. I always admired how well she did my pigtails and how hard she worked to make sure they always looked good. It was a job indeed in itself because my hair was so curly and so long. She worked with such precision every morning as she detangled and smoothed my hair into a new hairstyle every day. If only I had given her the credit then, but I was a kid. I didn't understand the love and dedication that she showed me.

I did not know much of anything. All I knew was that I wanted my hair to be straight and beautiful like most of the other girls at my school. Straight hair just seemed effortless. It did not matter what race they were. For some reason, I felt like everyone preferred straight hair, so I wanted that for myself. Looking back at it right now, I don't really think it was about the hair at all; it was about wanting to fit in and feeling like I belonged.

I don't remember how I expressed what I wanted to my mom, but somehow, she understood. I started getting my hair permed or, as some people say, relaxed. When I say it got my hair straight, I mean bone straight – there was not a wave or curl in sight. But getting there was not easy. It was a long and tedious process to get the job done. My mom had to part my thick hair in sections, apply the relaxer, let it sit, shampoo it out about five times, condition it, blow dry, and flat iron it. Each step took about forever and a lot of patience, but it was so worth it in the end. I loved the results every single time.

The first time my mom let me wear it down to school was so exciting. I felt confident and like I had stepped into a new version of myself. I could not wait for the other kids to see my hair. Maybe they would finally see me. The thing is, I did not have any friends. I usually just faded into the background. But that day, lots of kids came up to me and told me they liked my hair and that I looked pretty. They ran their fingers through it, and I could see the admiration in their eyes. One girl even started playing with it, twisting it between her fingers.

I was so happy with the attention I was getting, so caught up in the moment, that I didn't even realize my hair was now a mess. Strands were sticking out in different directions. When my mom came to pick me up that day, I slid into the car to hear her fuss at me about my hair being "all over my head." She was livid.

I did not see the issue at that time. In my head, it was harmless. I mean, they were just curious and wanted to touch it. What was the big deal? Plus, I was never the type to tell other kids no. I didn't know how. I wanted them to like me. If letting them play with my hair meant them accepting me, I didn't really mind it.

Now, relaxers wear off after a while, so I would have to get it redone quite often. Unfortunately, the straightness didn't last forever. Until then, I would wear my pigtails as usual. I was back to my hairstyle, but now much more aware of how different hair could make me feel.

Now, nobody necessarily said I looked bad with pigtails at school. It wasn't like they pointed at me or whispered about my hair. Well, there was one boy who told me I looked like a spider when I had eight pigtails one day. He didn't realize how much time and creativity it took to get my hair to look that way, but oh well. I laughed it off when he made fun of me. I forced a smile and pretended that it didn't bother me. But I still remember it like it was yesterday.

By that time, I was in second grade, so I knew more kids at my school, and they knew me. So, eventually, I did get comfortable in my own skin and my hair, for the most part. In the third grade, the school got more diverse. There were kids with new faces and new backgrounds all around me. I saw more brown-skinned girls, some who wore pigtails like me. This was exciting because I felt like I had someone that understood me. For the first time, I felt like I had someone who understood me.

Unfortunately, they were never in the same class as me. I'd usually see them in the hallways during recess or in the cafeteria, but I never got too close. I wonder if it would have made a difference if I had been close friends with someone like me. Would I have felt more confident?

Even when I saw those girls who shared the same features as me, I couldn't help but think that they were pretty and I wasn't. It didn't make sense. We looked alike, yet I felt like they had something that I didn't. So maybe it wouldn't have made a difference. Imagine being a child and never feeling content, even when life is good. Great life, a great family, great parents, good food to eat, good clothes and shoes, toys and games – I had it all. However, I did not know how good I had it at the time.

Why did I care so much about trying to be like other girls and wanting to be liked? Why did it matter what they thought of me? I obviously sought validation as a kid. I just didn't know what it was.

By the time I got to fifth grade, I no longer wore pigtails. I outgrew them and wanted to do something different. Instead, I started wearing my hair down in a ponytail or bun. Now, fifth grade was so fun. I found my place. I had a best friend named Jessica. She loved my name and she made me feel so normal, finally. I was sort of awkward before, but now I was just your average girl.

Jessica always told me I looked pretty because of my hair and skin color. The way she said it made me feel like she truly believed it. She was also a brown-skinned girl herself. She was so pretty and had such an outgoing personality. I admired her. On top of that, I felt super comfortable in her presence.

We walked home from school together and had sleepovers sometimes. Friendship with her seemed easy. Now Jessica had a boy in her class named Ori. He seemed like a sweet kid who apparently had a crush on me. One day, Jessica gave me a love note from him. It was decorated with hearts, birds, and flowers on it. He wrote about how pretty I was and asked me to be his girlfriend.

I had to circle my options, "Yes, No, or Maybe." Needless to say, I circled "Yes." My heart was racing, and I was super excited. I was so happy. How could I not be?

This was my first love and boyfriend. I fell in love with him so fast. I had never experienced someone being so into me, someone who told me day in and day out how pretty they thought I was. It was sweet.

Ori started walking home with Jessica and me after school. What started as two became three, and I loved every bit of it. Now, he and I lived further in the neighborhood, so we would walk to his house first, and then my house was down the street.

Jessica was in full support of our relationship. She was our biggest cheerleader. I remember when I would get mad at him over things I can't recall now. Jessica would bring me not one but two notes from him saying how sorry he was. Each note was filled with pretty drawings on them, too. That was definitely my boo.

Maybe he was the one I should have gotten married to. Who knows, right? As kids it felt like it was the kind of love that could last forever.

That year at school was great because of those two. Jessica and Ori made life so much better. Plus, for the first time I felt like I was somewhat pretty. That wasn't necessarily because someone told me; it was because I could finally see it for myself. I could smile at myself in the mirror, if that makes sense.

It's crazy because I could never point out any flaws I had when it came to my appearance, especially my face. Now I know there were none at that point in time. I was just a little girl who deserved to feel beautiful without question. If I had known then what I know now, things would have been so different. I would have been nicer and kinder to myself. I wouldn't have been so harsh on myself.

I had no clue that I was my worst critic. I guess we all are sometimes. I did not know how beautiful I was. But I do now.

Part 2

My middle school was across the street from the elementary school I went to. It was the same neighborhood, but everything felt different. A lot of kids I knew ended up going there, so at least I knew some people. That should've given me some comfort, but I couldn't help it; I was so nervous. I did not know what to expect. Middle school felt like stepping into a new world.

I just hoped to fit in somewhere. Ori and Jessica were there, too. But things weren't the same. Ori and I were no longer together. I was still friends with Jessica, but she had made new friends, and I guess I felt like they wouldn't like me, so I didn't try introducing myself. I was still very timid at that time and struggled to step outside my comfort zone.

On the very first day of sixth grade, I met a girl, Kianna, in my science class. She had pretty brown skin, wore glasses, had micro braids, and a pretty smile. But what stood out the most was something I could never forget. She had the most unique feature I had ever seen. It was her nose; something about the structure of it was so unique. I cannot put it into words, not even to this day.

We were coloring for an assignment that day. It was one of those simple icebreaker activities to help us ease into the new school year. She happened to be sitting across from me, thankfully, because I did not have colored pencils yet. She smiled at me and told me I could use some of hers. The small gesture really meant a lot to me.

We pretty much hit it off from there. Something just clicked. We became best friends so fast. Maybe it was because we both were shy and the kind of girls who observed more before talking. I guess it brought us together. We understood each other without saying too much.

We took on sixth grade together, and honestly, it was a lot of fun. We only had two classes together, science and history or whatever they called it in that grade. Whatever we went through that year, we had support from one another. We handled all our ups and downs together.

We walked home together every day. At first, I thought it was just convenient, that maybe our houses were close enough to make it make sense. She could have taken the bus, but she wanted to hang out with me. I did not know that was why she was not taking the bus until many years later. I knew she was a good friend for sure, though. She was the kind that stuck by your side even during the hard times.

I had such low self-esteem, and Kianna saw it before I even fully understood it myself. She was always trying to help me with that. She wanted me to see myself the way she saw me. I made comments about myself that were very negative, and she would correct me. She did not like it. The way I negatively talked about myself really frustrated her.

No one would like that or enjoy feeling obligated to give that confirmation to make that person feel better.

I had my good days, days when I could manage to smile at my reflection, but mainly days when I did not feel cute at all. I didn't know it was all in the way I carried myself. I always wore my hair in a bun, pulled straight back. I wore dark colors, like dark brown, gray and black. Those are not bad colors to wear, but the way I wore them was very dull looking. It did not help that how I felt on the inside showed on the outside. I just did not put effort into my appearance at all. Not because I didn't care but because I didn't see the point. I can't say I was too busy with homework to try new hairstyles or put together a cute outfit because, let's be real, I hardly did my homework.

If I had known then how much I would struggle with motivation, both in school and in making myself look presentable, I would have chosen to put effort into one of those things.

I definitely admired girls who were smart and pretty. The ones who seemed to have it all together. That's how Kianna was. She balanced both, and I looked up to her for it. You would think that I would have tried harder because I did hold myself to that standard. I wanted to be like that; I just did not execute. I wanted to do more for myself; I just didn't know how to. I could not do what I was supposed to do.

Once I got to seventh grade, I did just a little better. I didn't do anything drastic, just enough to feel like I was moving in the right direction. I remember having Mrs. Riverson for English class. I loved

Mrs. Riverson because she was so nice and so real. She treated us all equally and cared for us so much. She was the kind of person who made you feel seen. She and I had a special bond because we went to the same church. It felt good to have that kind of connection. She even let me call her by her first name sometimes, which was Angela. That alone made me feel special. She would pick me up for church on Tuesdays and Sundays. She even gave me Bible lessons on Saturdays.

She was like an additional mother to me. The kind of person who didn't have to care but did anyway. Sometimes, she would bring her husband, Gavin, to our Bible studies. He was cool, too. They were both like my mentors growing up. They didn't just teach me about the Bible; they taught me about kindness and other important things in life. That was proof that it takes a village to raise a child. I did not know how intricate that was for me at that time. How much their presence and words were shaping me.

Of course, they knew of my insecurities as well. How could they not? I remember even telling them I was "stupid and ugly" one time. They tried to tell me otherwise, but I guess it went in one ear and out the other.

Now, in Mrs. Riverson's class, there was one boy that made me hate that class. He made my stomach twist and turn every time I walked through the door. His name was Kevin. And Kevin had made it his personal mission to ruin my day. He made fun of me on a daily basis. He always had something to say about how I looked. He called me ugly all the time.

I got used to it eventually and even started to defend myself because what choice did I have? Until one day, he said the worst thing that I have never forgotten. One day, he looked at me and said, "Tebaliah, you're not ugly, but you're not pretty either."

At first, I was in shock because it was like he withdrew all the times he called me ugly. For him to say I was not pretty was only confirmation of what I already knew. I knew I wasn't ugly. But I also knew I wasn't pretty. It still hurt to hear him say that. Words like that don't just hit you and bounce off. They stay with you forever.

I was devastated because here I am, 12 years old, trying to look the best I can, and it was not enough. I think I gave up trying that year because there was no point. What was the use of putting in effort if the result never changed?

At least I still had Kianna. The one person who never made me question my worth. She was there and was always rooting for me to do better. She truly saw me and loved me for me.

Now, eighth grade was different. Something shifted. When it came to my appearance and my aesthetic, I did better. Some days were better than others. Some days, I actually liked what I saw in the mirror. There was this gray jacket I wore so much. It was kind of like my security blanket. I guess. It was comfortable for me and matched everything. However, Kianna got sick of it.

I usually pulled my hair back into a bun. It was quick and simple. No one would have known my hair was any longer. I did not have any issues with anyone making fun of me or calling me ugly. I had learned to blend in. I was definitely an awkward teen, but now I know a lot of us were to some degree. I had chipped my front tooth really badly over the summer. It wasn't a small chip, either. It was the kind of thing you couldn't unsee once you noticed it. It was blatant for people to see. Needless to say, I did not smile much that year. I was very insecure about my smile, and talking to people was hard.

I remember presenting my project in English class that year. I turned to the side and looked at my PowerPoint while I talked so nobody could stare at my teeth. I'm pretty sure they noticed anyway. No one ever mentioned it or asked me about it. But in my head, it was all they saw. I was sure that's what they were thinking about when they talked to me.

I didn't know it was all in my head. Once I got it fixed, I gained the confidence to smile again, and I felt so much better. That year actually turned out to be fun, especially towards the end. We went on a field trip to Schlitterbahn, the best water park ever. I remember wearing a cute top and shorts over my bikini at school that day. Everyone in my class kept telling me how good I looked. I blushed so hard, completely caught off guard. For the first time, they could see my figure. All those hours in athletics and walking home every day had definitely paid off.

At Schlitterbahn, when I took off my shirt and shorts, Kianna and the girls in our group gasped. They told me I had a bikini body and nice curves. By that time, my breasts were a good size, too, which was definitely a bonus.

The ride back from the trip was a thrill in itself. All I could think about was how amazing high school was going to be, the excitement of summer, and Usher's hit song playing on the bus. That summer, "OMG" was everywhere, it was stuck in my head for months. I was so ready to take on freshman year.

Part 3

Freshman year started on a bittersweet note. I had just broken up with my boyfriend, Travis – or rather, he broke up with me. It was the first week of school when he called and told me he loved me but did not feel the way he once did before. Just like that, he had fallen out of love with me.

We had only been together that summer, but I was a smart girl; I knew there was a disbalance in the relationship. I knew what it was. There were two new girls who had just moved into the neighborhood we lived in, and he started following them around like a puppy dog. When I confronted him about them, he would casually brush it off and act like it was nothing I should worry about. But I knew he liked them. I just did not want to lose him because he made me feel beautiful and loved. I didn't want that feeling to go.

At some point, he started dropping hints about being attracted to girls with a lighter complexion. That was not me. I was not his type. It felt like someone had stabbed me in the chest when he broke my heart. I couldn't shake the feeling that I was not pretty or good enough. I told my friends about it, and they tried their best to console me. It still hurt, though.

It was an unfamiliar pain, something I hadn't necessarily experienced before. Regardless, it turned out to be a great year for me. I took dance as my elective at school and had no idea how good I was until I actually tried it. It was fun and liberating and made me feel more confident.

Feeling I had finally found my passion, I tried out for the varsity team – and I made it. I was exhilarated. Nothing could bring me down. That summer, I had to take dance lessons and attend a three-day camp. It was hell.

It was fun as well, but imagine dancing all day and getting fussed at by the dance instructors just for grabbing water without permission. They knew we were exhausted. To this day, I don't know how I survived.

We learned several routines and performed them in front of the instructors and the other dance teams. Being on the team made high school fun. It also made me feel beautiful because I had to keep up my appearance like my mother advised. I put more effort into my hair and overall appearance.

Performing at pep rallies, football games, basketball games, and competitions gave me a rush like nothing else. I surprised myself because I had always been so shy.

Dancing helped me break out of my shell. For the first time in a long time, I could look in the mirror with pride despite my flaws. Kianna was so proud of me, and I was just as proud of her. She tried out for Colorguard and made the team. Colorguard is one of the most complex things I have ever seen, and the fact that she could perform those skills so well was beyond me.

During that time, we were finding ourselves. They say high school is what you make it, therefore, we tried to make it a great experience. At least for me, it was.

Junior year was even more fun. I met more people, started dating a new boyfriend named Josiah, and grew closer to a few friends on the dance team. Surprisingly, I actually enjoyed my classes at school, too.

The other kids were kind to me, and I got lots of compliments from people. For the most part, I made damn sure that I carried myself with confidence. People especially loved it when I wore my natural curly hair - they were amazed by its pattern. They would ask how I made it curly, and I would simply tell them, "Just water." It felt nice to be appreciated for my authenticity. Something that initially made me feel like an outcast now made me feel valued. I would still get my hair relaxed sometimes, but as soon as water touched it, it would spring back.

Technically, the curls were a relaxed version of my natural ones because of the relaxer. It was pretty, though. I just didn't realize it at the time. Now, Josiah did end up dumping me after a few months. It broke my heart, but I had to keep it together, especially since we had the same English class. That sucked so bad. The day after he dumped me over text, I moved my seat away as far away from him as possible. No way was I sitting near him after that.

I didn't know 16-year-old boys could be so cruel and insensitive. I understood why he left me, but I couldn't comprehend why he could not tell me to my face. Maybe he knew how vulnerable I was and was too scared to see me fall apart. All I knew was that I still loved him. What I did not know was that there were a few guys who had a crush on me the entire time Josiah and I were together.

There was Martin, Nathan, Marcel and Angel. I was oblivious to the fact that they even looked at me in that way. To me, they were my friends. I did not know they were crushing on me, and honestly, I could not see why they would like me. It was like trying to solve rocket science.

Senior year wasn't really as fun, mostly because I quit the dance team to focus on school work. I had slacked off pretty badly and I didn't want to face the consequences of that. I mean, yeah, I made A's an B's, but there were a couple of classes I almost failed. I had to do better and step up my game.

Thankfully, I had three off periods that year – four, technically, but one was for my student aide. I did my work that year, but my classes were hard, especially anatomy and physiology. That year, I mostly kept to myself. It was no fun at all.

I still made sure to look nice, but I was just there to get the job done, not to win a beauty contest. My least favorite class was AP Literature.

I liked my teacher, but everyone else in that class seemed way smarter than me. I felt out of place. The only thing I took pride in was scoring 100s on all my vocabulary tests. Each week, we were tested on college-level words, and I nailed them. I was proud of myself especially since my dad taught me to have a broad vocabulary growing up. It was a small win, but it meant a lot to me.

I guess I inherited that from somewhere. Of course, I graduated - Class of 2014. I remember graduation day so clearly. Kianna and I cried a little, overwhelmed with emotion. I was so proud of us. We had finally done it. We were walking the stage, receiving our diplomas, and in that moment, all those years in school flashed before my eyes. And just like that, they were behind me.

I knew I was a smart girl and that I would make something of myself. I knew life was just beginning.

For the most part, I was a nice girl, loved by friends and family. I just didn't know how beautiful I was.

The End

www.ingramcontent.com/pod-product-compliance
Lightning Source LLC
Chambersburg PA
CBHW051254120626
46547CB00014B/1936